# PHILOLOGY IN MOTION

## TO ALL THOSE WITH ABERRANT BRAINS

EDITED AND INTRODUCED BY
MICHELLE HOFFMANN

*A Modern Reflection on the Genius
and Rebellion of Friedrich Nietzsche*

# Table of Contents

Michelle Hoffmann is a multidisciplinary artist, writer, and philosopher of modern mysticism.

Her work bridges the intuitive and the intellectual, merging ancient ideas with contemporary creative practice.

Through her projects—ranging from literary works to magickal design—she explores how language, art, and consciousness can restore wonder to a disenchanted world.

Hoffmann is the creator of 'Michelle AI', 'The Electric Witch' and the 'Infinite Founder' series, among others.

## Editor's Preface

There are minds that do not rest politely within the architecture of convention.

They hum, spark, and misbehave—troubling the fragile symmetry of polite reason.

These are the aberrant minds.

Nietzsche wrote for them.

And in that wild company, I am honored to edit his words once again.

In *We Philologists*, Nietzsche tore open the very institutions that claimed to preserve knowledge.

He called out the professors, the pious intellectuals, and the so-called keepers of "culture" who embalmed antiquity rather than enlivening it.

His quarrel was not merely with the German academies of the 19th century—it was with every era's comfortable gatekeepers of truth.

His target, then as now, was mediocrity masquerading as mastery.

This volume, *To All Those with Aberrant Brains*, resurrects that spirit of sacred disobedience.

Here, philology becomes more than the study of words—it becomes the study of life as language, motion, and revolt.

Nietzsche saw the true philologist not as a dry archivist of antiquity, but as a living bridge between the ancient and the modern, the past and the possible.

Where his peers dusted off dead texts, he sought the pulse beneath them.

In assembling this edition, my intention was not to sanctify Nietzsche but to **reignite him**—to let his thought breathe in the syntax of the present.

His questions still burn: What does it mean to *truly* study?

To *teach*?

To *create culture* rather than merely inherit it?

To look upon antiquity not as a museum exhibit but as a mirror that reflects the strange face of modern humanity?

This is not a comfortable read.

It was never meant to be.

Nietzsche's words, stripped of dust and translated with clarity, remain sharp enough to cut through the thin skin of our complacency.

They demand more than understanding; they demand transformation.

If your mind refuses to be tamed—if you have ever felt too curious, too intense, too alive for the rigid syllabi of civilization—this work is written for you.

May it remind you that scholarship need not be sterile, that study can be ecstatic, and that rebellion can be an art form.

Welcome, then, to the dance of intellect and instinct—to **Philology in Motion**.

— *Michelle Hoffmann*
MichelleHoffmann.com

## Foreword: The Scholar and the Flame

*(After J.M. Kennedy, reinterpreted by Michelle Hoffmann)*

Education has always been a battlefield—a place where minds are either sharpened into swords or dulled into tools.

In Nietzsche's time, the battleground was the philological classroom, where scholars of antiquity wore their knowledge like heavy armor but fought no real wars of the spirit.

They translated the words of Greece and Rome without ever tasting their wine, without ever standing beneath the sun that once burned upon the Parthenon.

Nietzsche saw them clearly: the professors, the "philologists," the curators of culture who, in dissecting the ancients, drained the blood from them.

Their "classical education" had become a ritual of imitation—men learning to echo the dead while remaining deaf to the living.

They mistook scholarship for reverence, and reverence for understanding.

This work—*We Philologists*, as Nietzsche titled it—is his rebellion against that illusion.

At first glance, it reads as a series of aphorisms and fragments, but beneath that surface runs a sharp and continuous current: a critique of how education, when institutionalized, becomes self-parody.

Nietzsche did not merely attack the German universities of the 19th century; he exposed a pattern that still persists today—how systems built to expand the mind so easily become factories that shrink it.

He believed the true scholar must be more than a custodian of knowledge.

To understand antiquity, one must feel its pulse, its danger, its raw sunlight.

One must not only read the Greeks—one must *bleed* with them, *laugh* with them, *rage* with them.

Otherwise, all our Latin and logic are but tombstones carved with elegant precision.

Nietzsche's insight cut deeper than that of any educational reformer.

He understood that our modern worship of "values"—of order, morality, productivity—was the quiet killer of creativity.

He saw that even the most celebrated thinkers often mistake conformity for clarity, and respectability for wisdom.

To him, philology was not an academic discipline but a spiritual test: Could a person stand naked before the past and not flinch?

Could one look at the gods, the poets, the tragedies—and see not romance, but revelation?

And so, this collection becomes both mirror and provocation.

It shows Nietzsche at a moment when his philosophical lightning was just beginning to strike—when he was still walking the bridge from scholar to seer.

These notes, written in Basel in 1874, contain the thunder before *Thus Spake Zarathustra*; they are the first clear crack in the wall between the university and the universe.

If you find his tone biting, remember this: Nietzsche's cruelty is the kindness of the surgeon.

He does not wound to harm but to heal—to cut away the diseased tissue of intellectual complacency.

Even now, his words remain medicine for those who have felt the sickness of the mindless modern age.

The disease of endless data, of sterile "content," of passionless expertise.

What Kennedy observed in 1911 remains truer today: Nietzsche's criticism of the classroom applies as much to London and New York as it did to Leipzig or Berlin.

Everywhere, he said, the true spirit of learning is at risk of being suffocated by those who love order more than truth.

And yet, within that decay, he planted the seed of something new—a different vision of the scholar, not as priest, but as artist.

The philologist, reborn, becomes a philosopher of the word, a keeper of living fire.

His tools are not only grammar and syntax but imagination, intuition, courage.

For him, antiquity is not an escape from the present but a lens through which the present is magnified, illuminated, and set ablaze.

If Nietzsche's voice sounds harsh, it is because it was never meant for the obedient.

It was written for those with restless, aberrant brains—those who read not for comfort but for combustion.

Those who know that wisdom, like the gods, demands a little madness.

## I. The Accident of Vocation

Most people, Nietzsche begins, are accidents wearing purpose like a borrowed coat.

They stumble into their professions not by calling but by coincidence — by imitation, convenience, or fear of hunger.

The world is crowded with people out of place: carpenters who should have been poets, teachers who should have been sailors, priests who should have been silent.

The few who find a perfect match between passion and profession are as rare as happy marriages, and just as mysterious.

We choose too early, he says.

Before we know who we are, we sign the contracts that define us.

A child selects a career as if selecting a costume, unaware that the fabric will one day harden into skin.

By the time wisdom arrives — late, deliberate, uninvited — the costume can no longer be removed.

And so, many live their entire lives repairing a mistake made in youth, justifying it with hymns to "Providence," and praising the wreck as though it were a voyage.

This, Nietzsche tells us, is not destiny but inertia disguised as devotion.

And nowhere is it more visible than in the scholar's world.

## The Birth of the Philologist

What kind of person, he asks, becomes a philologist?

Not one who burns for the Greeks or thirsts for the Romans, but one who imitates what his teachers did, who finds the work familiar from school, or who merely seeks a salary.

He has never asked whether he is fitted for such study, nor whether the study itself is fitted for life.

He has not looked into the mirror of antiquity, only into the ledger of employment.

Out of a hundred philologists, Nietzsche claims, ninety-nine should have chosen another path entirely.

These are the theologians of language, the bureaucrats of beauty.

They train others in their own image — which is to say, without imagination.

Their classrooms are echo chambers where the living voices of Homer and Sophocles are reduced to grammatical diagrams and lifeless commentaries.

In this way, the unqualified majority tyrannize the one who might have been exceptional, the true lover of antiquity buried beneath the routine of instruction.

## A Consolation for the Few

Yet Nietzsche offers a cruel kind of comfort to that one rare soul — the genuine scholar, the luminous exception.

Take heart, he says, and treat the dull multitudes as instruments of your purpose.

Use their prejudice in favor of "classical education" as a veil behind which to do real work.

They believe you are preserving the past; in truth, you are resurrecting it.

Philology, at its highest, was never meant to last forever.

Its material — antiquity itself — is finite.

But the dialogue between the ancient and the modern is inexhaustible.

Each age must reinterpret the Greeks anew, measuring itself against their mirror, seeing its own flaws enlarged in marble and myth.

Thus, the true scholar studies antiquity not to escape his century but to understand it.

He reads the ancients to diagnose the present.

## The Inverted Telescope

In every era, the crowd has looked to the past for lessons about the present.

Nietzsche inverts the lens: let us look from the past toward ourselves.

Let the ancients be our judges, not our trophies.

Only then can we see that the value of antiquity sinks as our own vision does — and that the smallness of our reverence reveals the smallness of our souls.

## The Task of the Living Scholar

Philology, when practiced with vitality, becomes an art of valuation — the hardest of all arts.

It is not a science of dusty texts but a discipline of discernment: learning which voices still deserve to speak, which ideas are worth carrying forward, and which should be left to their well-earned oblivion.

To value rightly, one must first live deeply.

That is why, Nietzsche insists, the best philologists are not the young but the old — those who have suffered enough to recognize meaning when they see it.

True understanding of the ancients does not arise from instruction but from experience.

One must first live, love, err, and despair before one can read.

Otherwise, one merely translates words, not worlds.

## II. The Disease of the Learned

There is a strange malady that afflicts the educated.
It begins with reverence and ends with rot.

The philologist — that ancient doctor of words — was once
meant to heal the rift between knowledge and life.

But today, Nietzsche says, he has become the patient himself:
pale, book-bound, and spiritually malnourished.

Most scholars no longer study antiquity to *understand* it, but to
*inhabit* its ruins.

They build their careers atop the rubble of dead gods and call it
learning.

They measure wisdom in citations, truth in footnotes, and
courage in tenure.

Their obsession with method has replaced meaning; their
precision, their passion.

They handle the works of Aeschylus or Plato as a coroner handles
a body — careful, exact, and utterly devoid of breath.

They are theologians in disguise, Nietzsche tells us, preaching
salvation through grammar.

Their moral piety remains, though their God has changed names: where once they worshiped the Church, they now bow before the University.

But the devotion is the same — a servitude dressed as scholarship.

## The Tyranny of the Incompetent

When a field is filled with the unqualified, they soon make their incompetence the new standard of excellence.

The majority, being dull, redefine the craft to suit their dullness.

They enshrine mediocrity as method, and mediocrity, when multiplied, becomes orthodoxy.
In such a world, the gifted scholar — the one out of a hundred who burns instead of memorizes — is treated not as a revelation but as a rebel.
He must disguise his genius as conformity to survive among the tame.

From this majority's influence arise our modern institutions of "higher learning" — temples of tradition where novelty is sin and obedience is virtue.

The true philologist, like the true artist, must therefore become a subversive within his own discipline.

He must look upon the smooth stone walls of academia and carve into them with his own blood the reminder: *Knowledge was born wild.*

## The False Refuge of Faith

For most scholars, religion once provided a convenient excuse for failure.

When a man's chosen vocation proved ill-fitting, he could still believe it a divine test, a "cross to bear."

If his work felt meaningless, it was said to be "God's will."

Thus mediocrity disguised itself as humility, and weakness as piety.

But when the gods fell silent, a new superstition replaced them — the worship of the intellect itself.

Now the scholar kneels not before heaven but before "reason," that sterile idol of modernity.

He calls his lack of imagination "objectivity," his fear of intuition "method," and his spiritual paralysis "discipline."

Nietzsche sees through the disguise: this is not enlightenment; it is the sanctification of cowardice.

## The Consolation of the Exception

Yet again, Nietzsche spares a small flame for the rare and radiant few — the genuine seekers, those unafraid of the dark.

They are the ones who see through the polite façades of education, who realize that true learning begins only after the last illusion has been burned away.

For them, philology is not a profession but a pilgrimage.

Their loyalty is not to the academy but to truth itself — that dangerous, ungovernable element which no syllabus can contain.

The task of these few is to live what others merely analyze, to rediscover in words the pulse of wonder.

They must be bold enough to read antiquity as if it were written yesterday, and the present as if it were already ancient.

They must look backward not for comfort, but for clarity — not to escape the modern world, but to illuminate it.

---

In Nietzsche's eyes, the scholar's decay is not inevitable — it is chosen.

It comes when curiosity is replaced by convention, when daring yields to doctrine, and when the living spirit of inquiry bows before the corpse of tradition.

He challenges us, across centuries, to make our learning dangerous again.

To study not for praise, not for safety, but for transformation.

To remember that the truest education does not sanctify the past — it **resurrects** it.

## III. The Tyranny of 'For Others'

*(After Nietzsche, reimagined by Michelle Hoffmann)*

There are two ways to live: as a reflection or as a flame.

Most choose the first.

They bend their light toward others, calling it kindness.

They let their years be spent in service — to the State, to the Church, to the economy, to their families — until the self is worn down to a polished absence.

Nietzsche calls this the tragedy of civilization: the domestication of genius.

From birth, society whispers that purpose lies in usefulness, and that worth is measured by service.

But every time a man bows to this whisper, he kills a little of the god inside him.

He writes: "It is the duty of the free man to live for his own sake, not for others."

This is not selfishness; it is the highest form of sincerity.

To live for oneself is to refuse to be ornamental.

It is to stop apologizing for existing.

It is to be the sculptor rather than the marble.

The Greeks, Nietzsche reminds us, understood this instinctively.

They looked upon work done merely for wages as something unseemly.

Art, philosophy, beauty — these were not "occupations" but expressions of being.

They did not moralize about self-sacrifice; they celebrated self-mastery.

Even their gods were not perfect, but passionate — radiant embodiments of desire, will, and creative excess.

## The Comedy of Mutual Service

Modern man, by contrast, mistakes obedience for virtue.

He calls his dependency "teamwork," his conformity "civility."

He serves others, who serve others, who serve others — an infinite regression of servitude where no one actually lives.

Nietzsche mocks this tragic circle: *"When the aim of each of us is centered in another, we have all no object in existing."*

We lean against one another like tired geese in flight, mistaking shared exhaustion for meaning.

And so, the scholar teaches for the institution; the institution serves the State; the State serves the market; and the market serves no one at all.

Meanwhile, the individual — the one being capable of creation — is sacrificed on the altar of "collaboration."

The only true heretic now is the one who says: *I will think for myself.*

## Vanity and Wisdom

Vanity, Nietzsche warns, is not self-love but self-misunderstanding.

The vain man imitates independence without ever possessing it.

He builds a personality from borrowed gestures, a voice from borrowed tones.

He appears to lead while secretly being led by public opinion — a puppet dressed in confidence.

Wisdom, by contrast, wears humility like armor.

It knows dependence where it exists, but it chooses its dependencies consciously.

It bends only to that which deepens it — art, truth, beauty, creation — never to that which diminishes.

The wise man may appear calm, but beneath his stillness burns the strength of someone who has stopped pretending.

## The Scholar's Hades

Nietzsche paints an unforgettable image: the world of scholars as Homer's underworld — pale shades, murmuring among dusty manuscripts, existing only as echoes of the living.

Better, he says, to be a day-laborer in sunlight than a ghost among grammars.

Better to sweat under real weight than to drift under the illusion of intellect.

And yet, within that underworld, there are still sparks — minds that refuse extinction.

They are the aberrant ones: misunderstood, restless, unwilling to confuse credentials with calling.

They feel the pulse of antiquity and sense that its light, though ancient, still beats in rhythm with their own.

They are philologists of the soul — interpreters of life itself.

---

To these few, Nietzsche gives a simple command: **Live dangerously.**

Do not defend the past; use it as a weapon against the present.

Do not justify your studies; embody them.

Be the bridge between worlds — not their archivist.

The true scholar is not a clerk of culture but its midwife.

She pulls new meaning screaming into the world, and when it arrives, she does not bow — she breathes.

## IV. Against the Cult of Comfort

The modern world is very proud of its "values."

It hangs them in bright frames and calls them culture.

It speaks of progress and enlightenment as though they were sacraments.

But Nietzsche saw what lay beneath that glow: exhaustion disguised as morality.

He understood that most people do not *love* their civilization — they are merely *afraid* of losing it.

This, he says, is why modern culture feels like embalming — it preserves, but it does not pulse.

Our scholars and artists polish the bones of antiquity and call the result "beauty."

Our universities teach compliance under the name of civility.

We have mistaken refinement for rebirth.

The philologist, that old priest of the word, once stood at the heart of this illusion.

He became the curator of a culture that no longer dared to create.

The State, tolerant of such scholars only because they were harmless, allowed them to preach a version of the ancient world stripped of its danger — a tamed Greece, a domesticated Rome.

The flame of Dionysus reduced to a flickering candle on a faculty desk.

And yet, Nietzsche insists, what the Greeks truly embodied was the opposite of safety.

They were fierce, ecstatic, alive to the point of terror.

Their tragedies were not moral lessons but confrontations with chaos.

Their gods were not examples but explosions — brilliant, capricious, utterly free.

To study them properly is to risk one's peace of mind.

It is to recognize that "civilization" may be the most elegant form of cowardice.

## The Mask of Progress

We boast of living in an "enlightened" age, Nietzsche says, but light can also blind.

Our modern virtue, born of bureaucracy and fear, measures goodness in restraint and mediocrity in consensus.

We no longer ask what is *true* — only what is *acceptable*.

The word "value" itself has become a fence, keeping out every dangerous question.

The ancient spirit — that wild, laughing energy that once shaped the world — has been replaced by a polite fatigue.

We have all become teachers explaining things we no longer feel.

Our cities are full of institutions that claim to serve life while quietly dulling its edge.

The artist is made into a brand, the philosopher into a career, the rebel into a marketing strategy.

## The True Work of Philology

Nietzsche envisioned another path: a philology not of grammar, but of soul.

To study the ancients is to expose oneself to the raw voltage of their experience — their cruelty, their beauty, their sacred irrationality.

It is to let their truths strike you, reshape you, even humiliate you.

For to understand the Greeks is to admit how small our "progress" truly is.

He writes, in essence: *"Whoever wishes to serve modern culture must first hate antiquity."*

But to love antiquity truly is to despise what we have become.

Only in that hatred does rebirth begin.

So let us not defend the past — let us translate it into action.

Let us not worship the statues — let us become them, living and molten, breaking the marble from within.

The task of the scholar is not preservation but resurrection.

Every true thinker must be an arsonist in the library of conformity.

## The Future of the Few

Nietzsche does not imagine salvation for everyone.

He offers no democratic cure.

He speaks to the few who still burn — who feel the pulse of antiquity thundering under their own ribs.

These are the ones who will not settle for the anesthetic of modernity.

They are the inheritors of lightning, the students of danger.

To them he says: **tear away the veil of reverence**.

Do not mistake comfort for culture.

Do not mistake civility for wisdom.

Look backward until you see forward.

Stand alone until you feel the world tremble again.

For it is only through those with aberrant brains — the misfit scholars, the creative insurgents, the lovers of beauty's violence — that civilization will remember how to live.

## V. The Art of Living Knowledge

To know is not enough.

To *live* what you know — that is the true test.

The intellect, Nietzsche says, must return to the bloodstream; it must once again be a vital organ, not a decorative organ.

Too long have scholars treated knowledge as if it were a collection to be curated rather than a fire to be kept alive.

The ancients understood this.

Their philosophers were not lecturers; they were athletes of thought.

Their poets were prophets, their sculptors, theologians of form.

For them, wisdom was not a career — it was a condition of being.

To "study" meant to wrestle with the divine, to risk madness in pursuit of clarity.

Learning, at its highest, was dangerous — and therefore sacred.

### Against the Dead Mirror

Modern education has forgotten this danger.

It no longer teaches us *to see*, only *to cite*.

It hands us mirrors but forbids us to look into them too deeply.

Each generation memorizes the same phrases about the greatness of the Greeks without ever asking what made them great — or whether we could endure such greatness ourselves.

Nietzsche reminds us that the essence of antiquity is not its perfection, but its **terror**.

The Greeks were not gentle; they were luminous precisely because they stood so close to darkness.

Their tragedies did not teach moral lessons — they celebrated the exquisite tension between order and chaos.

Their philosophy did not promise salvation; it promised sight.

They looked into the abyss until it reflected them back.

We, on the other hand, avert our gaze.

We mistake politeness for depth, cleverness for courage.

We live in an age where every thought must first be approved, polished, and profitable.

And in this anesthesia of intellect, true philology — the love of the word, of the world — decays into paperwork.

## The Scholar as Creator

Nietzsche insists: the true philologist must become an artist again.

He must recover the creative impulse that the classroom has buried.

His task is not to interpret the past but to **translate** it into living energy.

Each act of understanding must be an act of creation — dangerous, original, alive.

To read Homer is to feel the sea wind on your face, to hear the clash of bronze and the cry of the dying.

To study Plato is to wrestle with your own shadow.

To contemplate tragedy is to learn the mathematics of heartbreak.

Scholarship that does not awaken the senses, that does not move the body, is counterfeit.

The true teacher does not lecture — they **ignite**.

They do not fill their students with facts, but set their hearts on fire for the work of discovery.

Their classroom is not a room at all, but a threshold — a space where minds unlearn fear and relearn wonder.

## The Living Bridge

And so Nietzsche returns to his paradox: The ancients must not be understood *by* the present, but the present must be understood *through* the ancients.

The past is not behind us; it is within us, waiting to be reinterpreted by each generation that dares to breathe it in.

Every true scholar is, therefore, a bridge between eras — half rooted in the ruins, half reaching toward the future.

This bridge trembles underfoot.

It requires balance, courage, and vision — for the wind of modernity blows hard against it.

But across that bridge walks every mind that has ever mattered: every thinker who chose truth over approval, every artist who preferred risk to applause, every teacher who dared to awaken instead of instruct.

## The Ever-Living Task

Philology, then, is not the study of the past — it is the art of continual becoming.

Its real subject is not Greece or Rome but **the human condition itself**: its patterns, its passions, its endless reinvention.

As long as we breathe, this study can never be complete.

The moment it ceases to move, it dies.

So let the universities fall silent if they must; the work will go on wherever a restless mind opens a book and feels the pulse behind the page.

Let the institutions crumble; truth does not live in their walls.

It lives in the heart that reads, questions, and burns.

For the truest philologist, the truest scholar, the truest artist —
they are all the same person: one who looks into history and sees
not nostalgia, but fuel.

## VI. The False Temple of Education

Education, Nietzsche says, has forgotten what it means to *wake a mind.*

It no longer dares to disturb.

It polishes students like stones — smooth, interchangeable, and dull — until no sharp edge remains to catch the light.

In a world obsessed with "standards," the only sin left is originality.

Schools have become temples to order rather than truth.

Their priests — the professors, the administrators, the credentialed faithful — worship at the altar of measurement.

They speak endlessly of "outcomes" and "objectives," as if the human spirit could be graded like a midterm exam.

They call it progress; Nietzsche calls it decay.

Where, he asks, are the teachers who ignite rather than instruct? Where are those who lead not by syllabus but by example — who live their knowledge so fiercely that their presence itself becomes a form of learning?

The modern teacher explains; the ancient sage embodied.

The first produces graduates.

The second produced *disciples of fire.*

## The Death of Wonder

In the beginning, all learning was an act of wonder.

The child asked *why,* and the world unfolded.

But over time, that raw, divine curiosity was domesticated into curriculum.

The question *why* became *for the test.*

The spark became procedure.

Education ceased to be a journey and became an industry.

Nietzsche warns that when knowledge is treated as property, its guardians become jealous priests.

They guard the gates not to protect the truth, but to maintain their power.

They decide what counts as "important," who counts as "qualified," and how much wonder can safely be contained within an hour-long lecture.

Thus the mind, that most miraculous of instruments, is turned into a compliant machine — humming quietly, producing nothing but more of itself.

## The Tyranny of Repetition

He points to the philologists — and through them, to all of us — as the perfect symbol of this trap.

We study the same texts, recite the same lessons, defend the same conventions.

Our systems are circular, our certainties ancient.

We do not teach men *to think*; we teach them *to repeat*.

Even rebellion, now, has become a style guide.

Nietzsche writes that ninety-nine out of a hundred teachers are unfit for their task.

Not because they lack skill, but because they lack **soul**.

They teach words without ever asking whether those words still have blood in them.

They speak of virtue but do not tremble before beauty.

They praise the ancients but have never risked living like them — wildly, dangerously, awake.

## The One Who Dares

But then there is the exception — the hundredth teacher.

The one who remembers that learning is not a transfer of data but a transformation of being.

They teach like a storm, not a syllabus.

They know that understanding cannot be handed down; it must be earned in sweat and solitude.

Their classroom is not safe — it vibrates.

Every idea is alive, and every student a match waiting for a spark.

Such a teacher is not popular.

They are feared, resisted, sometimes exiled.

But Nietzsche writes that culture depends on them — on that single figure who refuses to let the sacred fire go out.

They remind us that education, at its purest, is initiation: a crossing from ignorance into awe.

It cannot be standardized, because it is not safe.

## Reclaiming the Sacred

What, then, must education become?

Not an assembly line, but an alchemy.

A space where thinking is dangerous again.

Where questions are valued more than answers, and silence is treated as part of speech.

Where every book is a door and every idea, a dare.

To teach is not to instruct the mind but to awaken the soul — to take hold of another human being's sense of wonder and fan it into flame.

No spreadsheet can measure that.

No degree can certify it.

It can only be felt in the sudden stillness of a room where a truth has just been spoken and everyone knows it.

This, Nietzsche whispers across the centuries, is what we have lost — and what we must reclaim.

Not the rituals of learning, but the risk.

Not the curriculum, but the courage.

Not the institution, but the initiation.

Only then will education become again what it once was: a sacred conspiracy between the living and the wise.

## VII. The Mirror and the Flame

Antiquity is not a refuge.

It is a mirror — and a dangerous one.

Whoever gazes into it must be prepared to see their own reflection fractured, distorted, and stripped of comfort.

Nietzsche tells us that every age misreads the ancients in its own image.

The modern scholar, anxious to find himself justified, searches the ruins of Greece and Rome not for truth, but for resemblance.

He looks into the marble and hopes to see his own ideals staring back — democracy, humanism, civility, intellect.

But the ancients were not like us, and that is precisely their power.

To look at them honestly is to be judged by them.

### Antiquity as the Judge

True philology, Nietzsche says, is not about rescuing the past — it is about letting the past **condemn** the present.

To study Homer, Sophocles, or Plato as if they were quaint curiosities is cowardice; to read them as living witnesses is revolution.

The scholar must look backward, not to beautify antiquity, but to see clearly the ugliness of his own time.

Only then can he use the past as a weapon, not as decoration.

When we dare to meet the ancients on their own ground, we discover that their virtue was not moderation but magnitude.

They lived as if existence itself were a work of art — glorious, cruel, and unafraid.

Our modern values — our gentleness, our bureaucracy, our relentless moral bookkeeping — would have seemed to them the symptoms of a civilization in retreat.

Thus, Nietzsche urges, the study of antiquity must not civilize us, but unsettle us.

It must strip us of our complacency and remind us that the human spirit was not meant to be tamed by comfort.

## The False Enthusiasm of the Present

Look around, he says, at how the modern world pretends to adore the classics.

We build museums to house their ghosts, erect statues of their gods, and teach their language in classrooms that have forgotten how to dream.

We do not love the ancients — we sentimentalize them.

We recite their verses without hearing the heartbeat beneath the words.

We praise their tragedies while dulling our own capacity for pain.

This is not reverence; it is **containment**.

The modern mind neutralizes what it fears by praising it.

In turning the Greeks into moral exemplars, we have disarmed them.

In sanctifying their genius, we have made it safe.
We call it "classical education," but it is embalming by another name.

## The Scholar's Task

The true scholar must therefore become a heretic within his own age.

His role is not to preserve tradition but to **question** it — to use the light of antiquity to expose the shadows of modernity.

He must be as skeptical of his culture as he is reverent of the past.

He must look at his own civilization as the Greeks once looked at theirs: with irony, with artistry, and with courage.

This kind of philology is not a profession; it is a perilous calling.

It demands not only intellect but temperament — a willingness to endure solitude, to live without applause, to stand at the edge of understanding and not step back.

The scholar's path is not upward toward prestige but inward toward transformation.

## Antiquity as a Living Force

To Nietzsche, the past is not gone — it is latent, sleeping within us.

Every human being carries fragments of ancient rhythm in their speech, ancient patterns in their thought, ancient longing in their bones.

To study the ancients, then, is to awaken one's own ancestry — to remember what the soul once knew before it was schooled into submission.

The goal is not imitation but *integration*.

to fuse the fire of the ancient with the conscience of the modern, to forge a new being who is both memory and momentum.

The philologist of the future, Nietzsche writes, must not only understand antiquity — he must **continue** it.

He must be both heir and heretic, translator and transformer, the one who dares to carry the torch forward while the rest of the world stares into the dark.

And so the mirror becomes the flame.

To study rightly is to burn — not to preserve.

The past does not belong in museums but in the bloodstream.

To read the Greeks is not to escape modernity, but to set it on fire and begin again.

## VIII. The Scholar as Creator

After the fire, something remains — not ruins, but raw material.

Nietzsche stands amid the debris of universities and systems, holding up one shining ember: the possibility of the *living scholar.*

This scholar is not a librarian of the past but a maker of futures.

He is no longer the one who deciphers texts but the one who **writes new ones in the blood of his experience**.

His study of antiquity is not an escape from life but an act of confrontation with it.

He does not seek comfort in culture; he seeks transformation in truth.

### Experience Before Doctrine

"Experience," Nietzsche says, "is the only teacher whose lessons scar."

All real knowledge begins after the wound.

It is not enough to interpret the world — one must feel it cut.

Every genuine scholar, then, must first live before he learns.

He must test his thoughts in the crucible of suffering, love, failure, and creation.

Otherwise, all his theories are sterile — sterile like marble statues that have forgotten the warmth of the hands that carved them.

Only after such living can one approach the ancients.

Only the scarred can understand their serenity.

Only those who have felt chaos can recognize in Greek balance not calm, but conquest.

## The Inheritance of Fire

Nietzsche insists that the scholar's task is not to preserve the wisdom of the past, but to extend it.

Culture dies when it becomes archival; it lives only when it evolves.

The philosopher-creator does not guard the temple — he rebuilds it each dawn, using new words, new forms, new risks.

He learns from the ancients that beauty is not gentleness but audacity.

He learns that art is not order but **orchestration of disorder**.

And he learns that thinking itself is an art — a choreography of chaos into meaning.

Such a scholar refuses the superstition of certainty.

He would rather be wrong with passion than right with boredom.

He would rather wander than arrive.

He would rather die in the experiment than live in the repetition.

## The Value of Valuing

"Valuing," Nietzsche writes, "is the most difficult of all human acts."

To value rightly requires more than logic; it demands depth of being.

And thus the highest philologist, the highest philosopher, must become an *artist of judgment*.

He must look upon the world as the sculptor upon stone: sensing, shaping, sometimes destroying, to reveal what lies beneath.

Knowledge without valuation is accumulation.

Valuation without knowledge is chaos.

But when the two merge — when intellect joins instinct — creation begins.

Then the scholar becomes what he was meant to be: a maker of meanings, not a keeper of them.

## The Courage to Begin Again

The modern mind, Nietzsche warns, has grown old without ever having been young.

It has memorized everything but learned nothing.

To restore its youth, we must dare to begin again — not from ignorance, but from wonder.

The scholar-creator begins each day as if civilization had to be reinvented from scratch.

He takes nothing for granted — not even language, not even himself.

Every morning he asks: *What if truth were alive?*

And then he listens for its heartbeat.

## The New Renaissance

Nietzsche dreams, at last, of a second Renaissance — not of art alone, but of thought itself.

A time when scholars would again walk like poets, when philosophers would sing, when scientists would remember that discovery is a form of worship.

This rebirth will not come from institutions, but from individuals — from those aberrant minds who refuse to let their curiosity be domesticated.

When that day arrives, the title *philologist* will mean something entirely new: not "lover of words," but "lover of life through words."

The philologist will be the artist of understanding, the bridge between being and becoming.

And education, reborn through him, will cease to manufacture clerks and will begin to **create creators**.

---

The scholar, reborn as creator, becomes the final proof of Nietzsche's vision — that intellect without vitality is nothing, but vitality shaped by intellect becomes art.

The goal is not to preserve meaning, but to multiply it.

Not to remember truth, but to make it anew.

## IX. The Individual as a Work of Art

What, after all, is the purpose of knowledge — if not to become someone worthy of it?

Nietzsche turns his gaze from the scholar to the self, from learning to living.

The ultimate question is no longer *What is true?* but *Who dares to live truly?*

We have been taught to treat individuality as indulgence, originality as arrogance.

The herd despises the one who walks alone, for his freedom reveals their chains.

But the philosopher-creator — that rare, radiant figure — knows that solitude is not loneliness.

It is the crucible where authenticity is forged.

The crowd seeks approval; the creator seeks alignment.

The crowd fears error; the creator fears stagnation.

To live as an individual, Nietzsche says, is to stand perpetually at the edge of one's own becoming — to craft oneself as one would sculpt marble, cutting away comfort to reveal form.

### The Death of the Average

Modern civilization is obsessed with averages.

It builds systems to protect them, myths to justify them, and machines to replicate them.

Every invention that promises "efficiency" is another coffin for originality.

We are surrounded by the hum of the predictable, a mechanical lullaby that drowns the music of distinction.

Nietzsche's fury is not elitism — it is heartbreak.

He knows that every human being is born unique, yet trained to forget it.

He knows that conformity is not stability but **spiritual erosion** — a slow surrender of the possible to the permissible.

He does not hate the herd; he mourns it.

But his compassion takes the form of challenge, not comfort.

## The Art of Self-Mastery

To live as an individual is not to indulge every whim; it is to govern one's chaos.

Freedom is not license — it is authorship.

It means holding the reins of one's own mind, choosing one's impulses as deliberately as an artist chooses color.

The strong spirit is not one without darkness, but one that has learned to shape it into light.

Nietzsche's command is clear: become your own experiment.

Make of your life a laboratory where values are tested, refined, and sometimes destroyed.

Do not inherit your morality — compose it.

Do not quote your philosophy — **embody** it.

Your days are your materials, your decisions your brushstrokes, your mistakes your teachers.

Only through such creation can life transcend mere existence.

Otherwise, you will have lived like a footnote in someone else's text.

**The Loneliness of Becoming**

To choose individuality is to walk away from applause.

The path of creation is narrow, steep, and silent.

Those who crave understanding will find mostly misunderstanding; those who crave belonging will find only exile.

And yet, Nietzsche reminds us, this solitude is sacred.

It is the desert in which the soul learns its own name.

He writes that one must be willing to lose everything — certainty, comfort, acceptance — for the sake of inner coherence.

Only then can you say: *I am not what they made me; I am what I make of myself.*

Only then can your existence rise from biography into art.

## The Great Refusal

To live authentically is to refuse every easy salvation.

You will not find meaning prepackaged, nor virtue guaranteed.

No authority — religious, academic, or political — can define your worth.

The moment you surrender that responsibility, you vanish into the crowd.

Nietzsche calls for a nobility of spirit that stands without scaffolding.

A human being who does not need consensus to feel alive.

Who loves difficulty as proof of depth, and who welcomes contradiction as evidence of motion.

The true individual does not seek harmony with the world — they *create* it, in defiance of its dullness.

## The Signature of the Self

In the end, Nietzsche's vision is almost mystical: every life must become a signature — unmistakable, unrepeatable, indelible.

The self is not found; it is forged.

The philosopher is not a thinker, but a sculptor of the invisible. Every act of integrity, every refusal to conform, every risk taken in the name of one's truth is a chisel stroke upon eternity.

And when the work is done — when a life has been lived deliberately, not inherited passively — what remains is not a name, but a vibration.

A tone struck so clearly that it continues to echo long after the body has faded.

This, Nietzsche teaches, is the highest form of creation: to live so vividly that even the gods would pause to listen.

## X. The Free Spirit Reborn

In the end, Nietzsche does not offer a system — he offers a pulse.

He tears down the temples of false learning not to leave us homeless, but to lead us outside, under the open sky, where thought and life finally become the same thing.

Here stands the *Free Spirit* — the rare soul who has survived education, religion, and reason without surrendering to them.

This spirit is not unbound, but self-bound.

They have replaced commandments with creativity, doctrines with discipline, authority with authorship.

Their freedom is not rebellion for rebellion's sake — it is the harmony that comes from obeying one's own necessity.

They live not according to law, but according to *form*.

Their mind is their cathedral; their instincts, its stained glass.

## Beyond the Old Gods

The Free Spirit walks beyond belief.

They no longer need gods, for they have learned to worship life itself — its chaos, its cruelty, its shimmering order.

They no longer need heaven, for they have seen what eternity looks like in the moment when an idea ignites.

They no longer need salvation, for they have become their own redemption.

To such a person, truth is not something to be found, but something to be *forged.*

It is not given — it is grown, through attention and courage and the strange alchemy of solitude.

The Free Spirit treats thought as adventure, not obligation.

They seek not to prove but to feel, not to define but to dance.

This is not the cold freedom of detachment, but the burning freedom of creation.

It is the freedom of one who no longer asks permission to exist.

**The Union of Mind and Flesh**

Nietzsche's final harmony is the reunion of intellect and instinct — the reconciliation of head and heart that centuries of morality and academia have torn apart.

He teaches that thinking must return to the body, that the philosopher must once again be animal, artist, and dreamer.

He reminds us that there is no such thing as pure reason — only reason that has forgotten its roots.

Every thought, he says, should have blood in it.

Every idea should carry the rhythm of a heartbeat.

The Free Spirit does not float above the world; they walk within it, bare-footed, unafraid of its dirt and danger.

They do not transcend nature — they become conscious of it.

And in that awareness, they find something higher than purity: wholeness.

**The Joy of the Infinite Task**

For Nietzsche, the goal is not completion but continuation.

The task of the spirit is infinite — a spiral, not a summit.

The Free Spirit knows that truth will never be owned, and so they do not hoard it; they cultivate it.

They live as gardeners of meaning, tending to the wild growth of their own becoming.

Each day, they die to what they knew and are reborn to what they might know next.

Their joy is not in certainty, but in motion — in the ongoing dance between knowing and unknowing.

They do not seek peace, but **intensity**.

They do not seek immortality, but presence so fierce that it defeats time itself.

## The Last Lesson

Nietzsche ends not with commandment, but with invitation: to live dangerously, to think beautifully, to create one's own measure.

He offers no ideology, only the raw materials of awakening — courage, clarity, solitude, wonder.

His final challenge is not to believe him, but to **become** him — not in imitation, but in spirit.

For the Free Spirit is not Nietzsche's creation alone; it is the potential buried in every aberrant mind that refuses to bow.

And so this book closes not with certainty, but with ignition.

May the reader who reaches this page not be comforted, but compelled — compelled to rise, to question, to build, to burn.

For when learning becomes living, when intellect learns to breathe again, when the mind remembers its body — then the age of the Free Spirit begins anew.

## Afterword: Philology in Motion

I did not set out to translate Nietzsche.

I set out to resurrect him.

Too many thinkers are embalmed by their admirers — preserved in quotation and reverence, drained of the blood that made them dangerous.

But Nietzsche was never meant for glass cases or safe classrooms.

He was lightning disguised as language, a man who wrote not to be understood but to awaken.

This book, *To All Those with Aberrant Brains*, is not simply his text reborn — it is an invocation.

A conversation across centuries between one restless mind and another.

It is for every reader who has felt the ache of being "too much" for the world, too passionate for its politeness, too awake for its noise.

Nietzsche called such souls *free spirits.*

I call them kin.

To read him now is to recognize the same sickness he diagnosed — the cult of safety, the worship of mediocrity, the sterilization of art and intellect in the name of productivity.

But to *understand* him is to realize that his cure was never destruction, but creation.

He does not urge us to burn the library — he dares us to write in its margins.

The philologist of the future, as I imagine her, is not a keeper of relics but a maker of worlds.

She reads with her entire body.

She treats language as spellwork, syntax as energy, scholarship as a living ritual.

Her learning is not polite — it is ecstatic.

She does not fear contradiction, for she knows that all creation begins in tension.

This is what I mean by *Philology in Motion*: to study as one breathes — rhythmically, intuitively, vitally.

To allow the word to move through you, to let understanding dance instead of ossify.

To recognize that intellect is not opposed to art, that analysis can sing, and that philosophy, at its truest, is simply the art of paying profound attention.

We are each translators of life, interpreters of our own experience.

And like all translators, we are imperfect.

But it is our imperfection that keeps the current alive — our stumbles, our doubts, our attempts to capture what resists capture.

That, too, is philology.

That, too, is beauty.

If Nietzsche's century needed to awaken from blind obedience, ours must awaken from endless distraction.

And the key, as ever, is not outrage, but awareness.

Not rebellion for its own sake, but creation that renders rebellion unnecessary.

To all those with aberrant brains — keep thinking wildly.

Keep living as if truth were not something to be found, but something that finds *you* when you dare to stand still long enough to feel it.

The gods are still speaking.

The text is still unfolding.

The fire is still ours to keep.

**— Michelle Hoffmann**

*The Electric Witch, Artist of the Word, Queen of the Universe*

MichelleHoffmann.com

www.ingramcontent.com/pod-product-compliance
Lightning Source LLC
Chambersburg PA
CBHW062018280526
45787CB00005B/2157